MILLENIAL MYTHS

VERSES FROM AROUND THE YEAR TWO THOUSAND

Linus St. Pierre

APOTHEOISIS: A SONG

last night you were leaping among the stars;

this morning you are grey upon the coast.

in slumbering phantasm you rode wings

and moved between the celestial wars

in cygnus, so that darkness may not boast:

torn matter, who in wailing x-rays sings,

passes unknown through our scar beaten skies.

silver nocturnes sped your galactic hands,

yet solar dawn reduced you, and denies

that global bones, which burn upon these strands,

might arise to heavenly magnitude.

thus, intellect sees wakened eyes are wrong;

it knows your high battle for pulchritude

and harmony on the winged horse of song.

MYTHOI

I. Invocation.

Apollo,

vibrant youth of the lyre

concentrate our verse

on those affairs most precious

in the tempestuous judgements of men

and with satisfying melody

divert our obsessions into reason.

II. Bacchanalian

like an idol to the purple dome

and adolescent stars

in our junior year of high school

after the homecoming football game

against another far-off

autumn clad town,

on the hilltop

overlooking the street lights

III. Ulster

and when she had consumed the fish

it was heard within that country

above the football fields and the streams

a voice in song reminiscent of

the solitary waiting of tiny bells

and drunks akin to remote detonation.

LINES WRITTEN AROUND THE NEW YEAR

at the priest's winter party

your dirty blonde locks

were not present

though i half expected them.

NEAR WIRE FENCES

she has left trinkets, such as

house keys, bracelets,

and small bottles of ambergris,

in the decaying vegetation

that has overgrown her ancestors'

unsubstantial tombs.

when she awakens from the nightmares

where these assistances are accepted,

the clarity of concealment

is made evident:

the distance she stands from bereaved relations

is amplified in the disjunction of aeons.

None know the dead.
None know the hands that buried.

ARIDANE ON NAXOS

the night of the fireworks

when it was so hot that

we decided to put all

the chocolate in the refrigerator

at my house,

you were walking up the hill

from the strand in a loose dress

with a boy who had long hair.

BREAKFAST WITH MY FATHER

across the breakfast

paper reading table

from my father,

dishes, coffee cups,

i remember the story

the electrician told us

of his surprise

at hearing

the cicada's song

getting into his truck

that summer

EXPULSION

the loveliness of slender

apple trees is reduced to

a hallucination in the shuffling

of dusty footsteps.

the expression of the adored

moaning in the ears "exist departed."

disturbs every replicating filament

so that even the gentleness of consecrated fingers

must to an unarguable calendar cease.

you, would would arrest in a glass,

the red wines of france:

remember this song.

FROM THE FRENCH

the verse of

    a green worm

       towards

       a glass

DOCUMENT

the scandal of your lips

dry and barely pressing

the silver toes

of the crucifix

as if they were besmirched

with the living blood

while your family wasn't looking.

your ears straining to perceive

the clarity of

the medicine on his heart

taking on four bright

patterns of glowing sugar and light

so that all of us knew:

behold a saint!

CENTAUR

The faces
        of the girls
keep getting younger
along the college paths
after rainstorms

MICHAELMASS 99

when the nave

was cold, severe, and empty

you were there.

now we have music

and flowers

but your blue eyes

in joy no longer dance

around us

how i am saddened

that the girl who sat

in front of me

on holy thursday

in the year of the tiger

is distant; departed.

MARDI GRAS

fat tuesday

was hot

around the circles of the city

that made it an onion.

we danced through the grapes

and kissed the vine.

next, it was ash Wednesday

before we knew it,

like a picture of a submarine

that had spun.

how could you understand,

old bard, prophet of snakes

and man of bacon, how he put all

his symbols on her that night?

goddess of train stations,

chestnut buds, and lady pope.

they danced

like two wooden dolls

that reeked of musty rooms

and crumpled yellow tissues.

he did not intend to fold with the seasons but

It was cold and she drank tea

to soothe her stomach.

the small music

echoed like flowers

for days in my ears.

these shadows we use

to understand our passions.

ALBA FOR *MERCOLEDI DELLE CENERI*

the tea kettle and shark wander
over the horizon and set beyond the elm.
you hold my shoulder, and the air turns
purple in the winter cold. Clouds
escape from your nostrils. i want to touch
them too. They are the first sublimation
of departure.

when my maid arrives we turn back
the curtains of my bed, and grope
for your shirt, thrown on the formal chair.
though i curse the thrush for damage
to the grape, i do not damn the morning.
there is calmness in the solitudes to come and
our white city, stripped of embellishments.

CONSOLARE LYRA LUCTUM

a leaf

mute and falling

in november coldness

expires in a crash of golden

splendor

MAY DAY

I (rainbow over the town)

1) red.

nature is the focus of these thoughts

and songs without predictions.

chaos of the oak tree

and uncertainty

under the flower crowns.

rain comes like butterflies.

in the city we are given

to celebration.

hornpipes are passed from ancestors

in our brick apartments to honor the wet leaves.

2) green.

her hair curls the dance.

blonde.

II (transliteration)

let there be ashrams

and neoclassical opinions

to perform the imagery.

in the light that was created

through the begotten Word

receive these letters

o endless source of life!

Here dances the swan and the serpent

praised be He who in His

eternal age is youth;

who in the sublimity of his maleness

becomes the wombs of unkown beauty

with pollen painted faces

manifest in all things, even

her in whom I love Him.

then, praised be she, a butterfly

who ages and wrinkles with the

bean shoots, and the truth that

fragments in her existence.

she – the strand on which X

is suspended as thunder and yellow

in the may pole streams.

III (Allegro ma non troppo)

what is this tigerish flicker

on doug hill road when the beer

was free in the plastic cups?

Who is she in the thunder

when I left the car door open?

her thin body shivered with whiskey,

i remember.

she moves like a thousand clocks.
how describe a hand like hers,
her thinness of fingers?

the lunacy of a season:
so calm a night
and we were sitting in the
long thick growing grass
with cricket's chirp
and crackle bonfire.

then, the storm and
the hexameters opened up four ways.
she told me of the purple beaches
and how the dogs run there.
they shall compare us
to the sweet wines of the river
they have drunk.

we kids with sport and life
like the honeybee in rainstorms.
in the field house
we dance with the blossoms.

VERSE

the crisp leaves fallen in the parking lot

like turtles on the beach of our darkness

UBI SUNT?

You're gone.
Now even
the small garden wall
on which you sat
in other Aprils
is gone. Your soft
blue jeans, pink panties, red sweater
sizzle. Fried into the past.
They grey rubber on your sneakers
disintegrates into a memory.

HYMN TO DMT

O unimaginable and inarticulate eye
Of Horus who becomes
Alive
As the rose window
Above the altar of the Virgin
Hail to thee!

Because we know that you are sweet
And enduring with your
Endless flow of wisdom,
Because in your turning with night and day
For seasons and moths you are unchanged,
Because you bathe us in brotherhood
Like whiskey and prayer,
We bow before you!
Hail to thee!

Thou art the sound from the Hudson,
Osiris as he groans in his banks,
A group of poems called "The Coat of Arms,"
The central point of a song.
Hail to thee!

Thou art the solar disc of Re
With Latin written around him,
The halo of the Madonna
Which dwells in Heliopolis
The world inside a street lamp

After the closing down of public houses!
Hail to thee!

Because you have comforted our fathers

In times of wretched and prosperous peace,

Because you incite our mothers

In times of glorious and damnable war,

Because you are the throne to

The scent of celestial drama,

We bow before you.
Hail to thee!

Thou art the glow hieroglyphics,

The resting place of Pharos,

A tunnel of flowers to Truth.
Hail to thee!

Thou art the apex of pyramids in heaven

A leap to shafts of light from crystal,

The hum of mediaeval stones,

Hail to thee!

Because you are an unburst reservoir of commerce,

The gossip of angels symbolic and physical,

Because thou art more beautiful than a thousand breasts
Because you show us the loneliness

Of Aten in his hairy orbit,

We bow before you.

Hail to thee!

Thou alone art cyberspace!
Hail to thee!

AN ANATOMY OF THE WORLD

blackness of ink on the page

when i read your name in the paper.

what I remember for three days,

all that i can think about,

during april nights

before your burial

is how when we were thirteen

you cooked pastries

for our french class but

forgot to sift the flour.

ARTEMIS' BATH

like tenth grade biology in September

with the daring to glance at the

strange and new pretty girl

across the classroom whose pale

skin made me wonder where

she had been all summer

ENDYMION

the silent moon across the sky
casts no light upon me.
but when she descends to my rooms
pale dreams pierce my body.

in these deep scenes i do not rest:
i ride and hunt with her.
though i am frozen in endless youth,
i burn within my slumber.

"THE BRITTLE IS EASILY SHATTERED"

+a dream from the isle of the dead+

like a dance along the lawn.

i see you for the first time this summer;

your hair is so short now

in the eastern sunlight.

i wave.

you smile over your shoulder,

change direction, like an athenian chorus

and step toward me.

then, you hesitate (as the small birds

assemble their song), turn back,

and walk away

past the crab apple trees in blossom.

when i awaken it is winter.

TO THE TUNE OF "THE GALLANT BOYS OF WESTPORT"

as if there was no first morning

after her refusal.

another summer comes

and he dreams that

he still has time to win her

as if nothing passed.

as is she were

a prize at the fair.

Lord, save us from the folly of young men.

PRELUDE FOR A STORY

only at evening time

when the girl with black hair

would come and wait on tables

in the lush holiday of May

and set wine and sausage

before us in the open air

only then,

and not in whispers

ORPHEUS AFTER THE UNDERWORLD

decked

with cherries and pomegranate

he dreams of her

still with long hair

splashed over her collar

and translucent arms

in the morris dance

SOUVENIR

four years of absence.

then one day on an arched bridge

you pass – teeth still white,

taller, wearing a salmon dress.

my face is not recognized.

FLOWER INTOXICATION

wild hum

of summer bees

around dry house gutters;

on stone patio you water

tulips

YSOLDE

she calls with whistles

and harp strings

with the ornate designs

carved in sold whiteness

to words inscribed

on their bodies like moist pearls

or the first sips of wine

when evening begins.

like the swan sequence,

stately and slender she moves

toward him.

he has tumbled with fresh

green weeds into

a wet ditch

called love.

MAENADS

rose colored wine, in the spring, they will drink,

ladies with strong hands that fracture men's bones.

concentrating on their god's ecstasy

they will be carried off by his flute tones

to the night-forest and bonfire by sea

with raptures that leave ripened cheeks still pink.

to the groves of Apollo came this dream,

where I dozed in the green shades before tea.

this odd vision did not expire nor sink,

and the meaning disturbs me still with moans,

haunts me to drop my spoon and spill the cream.

i look with innocence on mountain stones

no more, but of violent dances think.

those bright eyes are more brutal than they seem.